P9-CMP-755

BARACK OBAMA

COLEEN DEGNAN-VENESS

Level 2

Series Editors: Andy Hopkins and Jocelyn Potter

LONGWOOD PUBLIC LIBRARY

Pearson Education Limited
Edinburgh Gate, Harlow,
Essex CM20 2JE, England
and Associated Companies throughout the world.

ISBN: 978-1-4082-3165-4

This edition first published by Pearson Education Ltd 2011

3 5 7 9 10 8 6 4

Text copyright © Coleen Degnan-Veness 2011

Set in 11/14pt Bembo
Printed in China
SWTC/03

The moral rights of the authors have been asserted in accordance with
the Copyright Designs and Patents Act 1988

*All rights reserved; no part of this publication may be reproduced, stored
in a retrieval system, or transmitted in any form or by any means,
electronic, mechanical, photocopying, recording or otherwise, without the
prior written permission of the Publishers.*

Published by Pearson Education Limited in association with
Penguin Books Ltd, and both companies being subsidiaries of Pearson PLC

Acknowledgements
The publisher would like to thank the following for their kind permission
to reproduce their photographs:

Getty Images: 13, 19, 24, Time & Life Pictures 11, Washington Post 1;
Photoshot Holdings Limited: UPPA 4; **Press Association Images:** AP / Obed
Zilwa 16; **Reuters:** Obama For America / Handout 7
Cover images: *Front:* **Press Association Images:** AP / Mannie Garcia

All other images © Pearson Education

Every effort has been made to trace the copyright holders and we apologise in advance
for any unintentional omissions. We would be pleased to insert the appropriate
acknowledgement in any subsequent edition of this publication.

For a complete list of the titles available in the Penguin Readers series please go to
www.penguinreaders.com. Alternatively, write to your local Pearson Longman office
or to: Penguin Readers Marketing Department, Pearson Education,
Edinburgh Gate, Harlow, Essex CM20 2JE, England.

Contents

Introduction

"Yes we can!"

When Barack Obama started his presidential campaign, a lot of people asked questions about his past jobs. Did those jobs really make him ready for the most difficult job in the world? What did he know about politics? But when he was a community organizer, a lawyer, and a young senator, Obama talked to the best people in government. He listened to their ideas, and he learned from them. He understood politics and political campaigns.

Americans want a strong president. He has to stand tall in the eyes of the world. People want him to do the right thing, without mistakes. In many ways, Obama is the right person for the job: He is a quiet, disciplined, and intelligent man. He thinks. He listens. And he almost never gets angry.

Obama's mother taught him about Martin Luther King, Nelson Mandela, and Mahatma Gandhi. (You can read their stories in Penguin Readers and Penguin Active Reading.) King gave his life for a better life for African-Americans. Mandela fought the South African government because black people there were not free. Gandhi's work made people in India free from the British. Obama wanted to bring hope to poor people, but first he had to change his country. He wanted to give hope for a better future to all of the American people. When they asked, "Can you do it?" his answer was always the same. "Yes we can!" It was not a job for one man; it was a job for everybody.

Chapter 1 The First African-American President

Early on the afternoon of January 20, 2009, Barack Hussein Obama, at the age of 47, started the most difficult job of his life—he was the 44th president of the United States. Every four years, American presidents start their time in office on this date. But 2009 was different, very different. For the first time, the country had an African-American president.

His election changed the future of the world's most powerful country. A person's race can never again kill their hopes of the country's top job. The election of a black man gave hope to many black Americans, and to many other Americans, too. On that very cold day in 2009, Obama stood in front of almost 2,000,000 people in Washington, D.C. Mrs. Obama stood next to him, and he repeated the famous words with his left hand on the Bible.

Barack Obama puts his hand on the Bible.

In 1861, Abraham Lincoln, America's 16th president, put his left hand on the same Bible when he started his presidency. Lincoln was a very important president in the story of African-Americans. From 1861–65, Americans in the North fought a war with Americans in the South. When it ended, black people were free. After that, they did not have to work for no money on white people's farms. But they could not get good jobs or good houses. Black people worked and fought for a better life for many years.

On that January day, Obama's wife and two young daughters watched him, and the world watched on TV. It was the day after Martin Luther King Day. King was another famous black man with dreams for African-Americans. On August 28, 1963, King spoke to more than 250,000 people in Washington, D.C., about a better world for every American. He wanted better homes for black people and better jobs, too. Forty-five years later a black man had the most important job in the country, and his family moved into the White House, the country's most famous home.

President Obama spoke to Americans about the many problems in their country: problems with the economy, the wars in Iraq and Afghanistan, the problems for sick people without money for hospitals, and the bad schools for children from poor families. He talked about past times, better times, and about hope for the future.

"It will not be easy," he said. "Our government has to use money carefully and make intelligent plans. A country cannot be rich when the government helps only rich people." He remembered the Americans in Iraq and Afghanistan. "Their work is a lesson for all of us. Now, every American has to work for this country."

But how did Obama win the presidential election?

There were eight Democratic* presidential candidates after

* Democrats and Republicans: the two most powerful political parties in the United States government

Obama put his name with the other seven on February 10, 2007. One was Hillary Clinton, the wife of President Bill Clinton (1993–2001). Later, the winner had to get more votes than the Republican candidate. Many Democrats wanted Hillary Clinton to win and to be the first woman candidate. American election campaigns cost a lot of money, and the Clintons had more money than Obama. The candidates have to pay a lot of people for their work on the campaign. They have to pay for television time, too. Obama organized Democrats across the country. He and his workers asked Americans for money for his campaign. In the end, Obama got more than the Clintons and on August 28, 2008, he won.

The Republican candidate, John McCain, was a famous white senator from Arizona, age 72. A lot of people liked McCain—but was he too old? Was Senator Obama from Illinois too young? Age was important. But race was more important for many people.

Who was this tall, thin black man with a funny name? Not many people knew Obama before July 27, 2004, when newspapers and magazines started to write about him. On that day, the Democrats met in Boston because Senator John Kerry was their new presidential candidate. Kerry had to start his campaign, and he wanted a good speaker. He invited the young black senator from Illinois, Barack Obama. When Obama finished speaking, the Democrats were excited. The American people watched him on TV and they liked him, too. Everybody wanted to know more about him. "Can he be a future president?" people asked. Suddenly, a lot of people bought his book about his early life, *Dreams from My Father*. It did not sell very well in 1995 but in 2004 it sold quickly. Obama was a lawyer and he taught law at a famous college in Chicago. But the book made him a rich man, not his jobs.

In 2008, Obama used the words "Hope," "Change," and "Yes we can" in communities across the country, and people loudly repeated the words after him. The country wanted change— and it got it.

Chapter 2   Early Life in Hawaii and Indonesia

President Barack Obama's father, Barack Hussein Obama, Sr.*, worked on his father's farm in Kenya, in Africa, when he was a boy. He was smart and, in 1959 at the age of 23, he wrote to a college in Hawaii. The college gave him a free place and he studied economics. He was their first black student. There, the next year, he met Stanley Ann Dunham, age 18, a white student from Kansas. Stanley Ann had her father's first name but people called her "Ann." They married. On August 4, 1961, their son, also Barack Hussein Obama, was born in Honolulu, Hawaii.

Stanley Ann Dunham and Barack Obama, Sr.

★ Sr.: short for "Senior." When a son's name is the same as his father's name, the father puts Sr. after his name.

In the United States in 1961, white people did not often marry black people, and in some places it was dangerous. But Hawaii, 3,200 kilometers southwest of California in the Pacific Ocean, was the newest state, and there were people of different races there. But not many black people lived there at that time. Stanley and Madelyn Dunham were not very happy about their young daughter's African husband but after a short time they liked him. And they loved their grandson. The family called the baby "Barry," an American name.

In 1963, Harvard, a very important college in Massachusetts, gave Obama Sr. a free place in their economics classes. Obama Sr. was very happy because Harvard was the best college in the country. When he left Honolulu, Ann and Barry had to stay there. Harvard did not give him money for his family.

In 1964, Ann's married life with Obama Sr. ended but she did not stop writing letters to him. She talked about him often to Barry. Obama Sr. was free again, so he married another white American woman in 1965. His second American wife, Ruth, was really his third wife. In Kenya, his first wife, Kezia, waited for him with their two children, Roy and Auma. Obama Sr. took Ruth to Kenya, and had a very good job in the government for some years. He visited Kezia, too, and had two more children with her.

Ann's mother and father met in Kansas but they did not live there for long. In World War 2, Stanley Dunham fought in France. After the war, he moved his family to California. Then they moved back to Kansas, then to Texas, and then to Seattle, Washington, so young Ann never had many friends. In Seattle she finished her high school education but, in 1959, Stanley's company sent him to Honolulu. The family moved again. He worked in a store and Madelyn worked in a bank. They did not have a lot of money but they were not poor. Ann loved books about people from other countries. She read as many books as she could. This gave her ideas for her future. She wanted to

5

learn about people in poor countries. She wanted to help them. Years later, she helped poor people in Indonesia.

Obama's early life in a white family without his black father was not the best life for an African-American boy in the early 1960s. He looked different from the other children, but he did not know about racial problems in his early life. He did not know his African and African-American brothers and sisters in Kenya but his white family loved him very much. Ann was a very intelligent woman with big dreams for her future, so she went back to college. She studied and started a new life.

Ann met an intelligent and kind young man at college, Lolo Soetoro, from Indonesia. Lolo visited the Dunham family often, and Ann's parents liked him. After two years, Ann and Lolo married. But there were problems in the Indonesian government and, suddenly, Lolo had to go back to his country. His government sent him to New Guinea, so he could fight in a war there. About a year later, he went back to Jakarta, and Ann and Barry moved there.

In his book *Dreams from My Father*, Obama remembers his first day in Jakarta: "There were strange, wild animals in the yard behind our new house. My mother and I jumped when we saw a big, hairy animal with a small head and long arms in the tree. Lolo told us, 'His name is Tata. I brought him from New Guinea for you.'" It was an exciting day for the young boy and he was very happy in this new world.

Barry went to a Catholic school for three years. He learned the Indonesian language and he had friends. His teachers say that he was a kind, quiet boy. When Lolo got a better job, he bought a bigger house. So Barry had to move to a new school, a Muslim school. Ann taught her son for three hours every morning before he went to school. Barry did not like getting up at four o'clock in the morning but his mother wanted him to have a good education.

In 1970, Barry's sister, Maya, was born. Ann taught her children a very important lesson in life—a person's color is not important. She wanted her children to be good, kind people, so she taught them about churches. One day, Barry's teacher asked her class about their plans for the future. They wrote their answers. Years later, she told people Obama's answer: "He wanted to be president. He didn't say of what country ... but he wanted to make everybody happy."

After three years, Ann was unhappy with Barry's education. She was unhappy about Lolo's job, too. Lolo worked for an American company, and he wanted Ann to like these people. But she did not like them or their parties. She wanted to talk to Lolo about the government and the problems of poor Indonesians but he did not want to discuss these things. Lolo wanted more children but Ann did not. Their happy family life ended.

Lolo Soetoro with Ann, Maya, and Barack in Indonesia.

Obama wrote about this time. His mother wanted him to go back to Honolulu and study at Punahou, a very good, expensive school. In 1971, Barry went back to Hawaii. Stanley and Madelyn met their grandson at the airport and took him home with them. But now they lived in a small apartment. At this time, his grandmother had a very good job in the bank and it paid her well. But his grandfather's new job did not pay him very well. Punahou paid for some of Barry's education but the money from Madelyn's job was important, too.

It was almost Christmas in 1971 when Ann left Lolo. She took Maya back to Honolulu with her. Barry had another visitor that Christmas—his father. This tall, very black man spoke British English, and he had a bad leg.

Obama Sr. was not very well at this time after a car accident. But he was happy when he saw his son. Barry could not feel love for this stranger, so it was a difficult month for him. Obama Sr. stayed in the apartment below the Dunham's apartment but he tried to change their lives. He wanted his son to study more and not to watch TV. After an angry conversation about a movie on TV one evening, Barry wanted his father to leave. But Obama Sr. stayed for Christmas, and he gave his son a basketball. He wanted Ann and her two children to go back to Kenya with him but Ann said no. She had other plans. She wanted to study. She knew about Obama Sr.'s two wives in Kenya and his sons and daughter, and she did not want to live with them.

The children at Punahou came from rich families, and most of the children were white or Asian. Barry began to understand about different races. Ann taught him about the problems of African-Americans and the work of Martin Luther King. And she taught him about Nelson Mandela and the problems of black people in South Africa. Ann wanted people to be free in every country, and she wanted her son to be happy with his color. She also wanted him to do good things for the world.

In 1977, Ann went back to Indonesia for her college work and she took Maya. Barry did not want to go, so he stayed with his grandparents. Barry's school friends remember him well. "He was tall and played basketball very well. He was friendly and kind," they say. But without a mother or father's discipline he did not study long hours. He loved basketball and he could play behind his grandparent's apartment. But these easy days in Hawaii ended when he finished studying at Punahou.

Chapter 3 Community Organizer and Law Student

After Barry finished high school, he studied at Occidental College in Los Angeles for two years. Occidental sent some of its students to Columbia, a very important college in New York City. Barry wanted to study there, so in 1981, he went to New York. He lived in Harlem, in a black community for the first time. Barry began to change and he wanted people to call him Barack, his African name. He read a lot of books and was a disciplined student. He did not have time for parties and he had little time for basketball.

After Obama finished his two years at Columbia, he had to find a job. He had to pay back to the bank the money for his education. In New York, he got a very good job in a large company. But Obama wanted to help poor people, not rich people. He read about community organizers and he liked their ideas. They worked with poor people in their communities and organized campaigns for change. He, too, wanted to be a community organizer, so he sent a lot of letters to community organizations. He asked for a job but nobody wrote back. Then one day, he got a phone call from Jerry Kellman. Kellman wanted to send a community organizer to Chicago, Illinois. Kellman met Obama and gave him the job. This was Obama's dream.

In south Chicago, the largest community of blacks in the United States, Obama saw a lot of angry men with no jobs. Not everybody was poor but there were a lot of problems in the city. Obama read books and learned about the important work of a community organizer. He listened to people and learned about their problems and their hopes for the future. He tried to work with the churches but the powerful men in the churches did not want his help. He was not from their community, and he had a college education from white people's schools. Obama organized poor black people in south Chicago and they made some changes for better houses. He wanted to put power in the hands of the poor people. But without a better education, he could not do more for Chicago's black community. Obama had to study law.

◆

One day in November 1982, Obama got a phone call from a stranger—his aunt in Nairobi.

"I am your Aunt Jane. Your father is dead," she told him.

After a night with friends in a bar, Obama Sr.'s car went off the road and into a tree. He died in Kenya at the age of forty-six. Obama did not know his father very well and he did not feel very sad. But when he phoned his mother, she cried.

A short time later, Obama's African sister, Auma, visited him in Chicago for the first time. She told her brother about their father's problems before he died. When she was young, his job with the Kenyan government ended suddenly. He did not like some of the people with political power, and he told other people that. When the government took away his job, he started drinking in bars. His American wife left him and she took their two sons. He had almost no money.

Obama listened and made some important plans for his future. He did not want *his* life to follow the mistakes of his father's life. He wanted to have a better future, and he wanted to help other people.

♦

At the age of 27, Obama began studying at Harvard Law School. He was a disciplined student, intelligent, and friendly with everybody. He told students, and teachers, his ideas for a better life for the country's poor people. Obama was older than most of the other students, and his teachers enjoyed their conversations with him. After his first year at Harvard, Obama got a summer job in a law office in Chicago. He worked with a young, black lawyer, Michelle Robinson. She had to help him with his work because he was only a law student. She had to teach him, and she was not excited about this.

Years later, Michelle said, "Before he arrived at the office,

Barack Obama at Harvard

everybody talked about this young African-American. To me, he was only a first year student with a funny name."

Obama liked Michelle because she was intelligent, interesting, and beautiful. He wanted to go out with her. But she said no. She said later, "We were the only two black people in the office. I didn't want people to talk about us. It wasn't right."

But Obama did not stop asking her. He sent flowers and notes, and he called her on the phone. At last, one Sunday, he took Michelle to a church in south Chicago. When he spoke to some poor African-American mothers, Michelle saw a different man, a very kind man. But he had to ask her many times before she went out with him. "You won't be sorry," he told her. He took her to a movie about racial problems, *Do the Right Thing*. At the end of that evening, Michelle found something new in her life—love. But she wanted her older brother, Craig, to play basketball with Obama because Craig, a basketball teacher, understood players. "You can learn a lot about somebody from their game," said Craig. He watched Obama carefully.

After they played, Craig said very good things about Obama. "He works well with the other players, and he's not afraid. He wants to win," Craig told Michelle. About a year later, in the Robinson's house, Obama told Craig, "I want to be a politician. Maybe one day, I can be president of the United States." Craig looked around the room. "Don't tell anybody that," he said. "What a crazy idea!" he thought.

Obama went back to Harvard in September, and the law students elected him to a very important job—president of the Harvard magazine for law students and lawyers in the United States. He won the election because he listened to people. He was the first African-American president in more than one hundred years, and the *New York Times* and the *Los Angeles Times* newspapers wrote about him. This opened a new door to his future.

Chapter 4 The Obama Family in Kenya

Before Obama started studying at Harvard Law School, he flew to Europe on his way to Kenya. He wanted to meet his African family. He visited London, Paris, and Barcelona. But he was a stranger in strange countries, he felt. After three weeks in these and other European cities, he arrived at the airport in Nairobi. For the first time in his life, he was in a country of black people. He was not different, and people there knew the name Obama very well.

Obama wrote about this important visit. Everybody in his large family was friendly. Some people spoke English but some did not. He met his father's first wife, Kezia, and her three sons—Roy, Abo, and Bernard. Obama stayed with Kezia's daughter, Auma, because he knew her from her visit to him in Chicago.

Standing left to right: Uncle Said, Barack, Roy (Abongo), friend, Abo, Bernard. Sitting: Auma, Kezia, Sarah, Aunt Jane

Roy lived in Washington, D.C., and he flew to Kenya, too. He wanted to meet his American brother. Obama also met his father's third wife, Ruth, and one of her two sons, Mark. (Her other son, David, died in a car accident in 1983.)

Obama Sr.'s youngest son, George, was born in 1982. George's mother, Jael, lived with his father but she never married him. At that time, there was a different government in Kenya, and Obama Sr. had a good job again. His life was better. But it ended suddenly in a car accident when George was only six months old.

Auma took Barack to their grandfather's farm in Kogelo, near Lake Victoria, and there he met his grandfather's third wife, Sarah. She did not speak English. So Auma listened and she told Barack Sarah's story:

Auma and Barack's grandfather, Onyango, was born before white men came to Kenya. When he was a boy, he did not play with the other children. He was a strange child, and he could not sit quietly. There were no schools but he learned about flowers from a neighbor. The neighbor helped sick people, and Onyango learned from him. Later, when white men arrived in the city of Kisumu in the west of Kenya, Onyango walked 40 kilometers there from Kendu. He wanted to see white people, and he hoped to learn English. Many months later, he went back home in white men's clothes. His father told Onyango's brothers, "Do not go near him." Onyango went back to Kisumu and never spoke to his father again. Some years later, a white man in Nairobi gave Onyango a job in his house. Onyango walked for more than two weeks to Nairobi. He cooked for the white man, and he organized his house. He worked for other important white men, too. When he had a lot of money, he bought a farm in Kendu, but not near his father's farm. Onyango's first wife, Helima, could not have children, so he married another woman, Akuma. She was the mother of Obama Sr. Later, he married Sarah. In World War 2, Onyango cooked for the British in Burma (now Myanmar), Ceylon (now Sri Lanka), the Middle East, and Europe. After three years, he went back to Kendu. Not long after that, he moved his three wives and children to Kogelo, 60 kilometers northwest of Kisumu, and there he had a very good farm. He gave a lot of the food from his farm to his neighbors. But Akuma was very unhappy, so she left her husband and two children. Barack's father wanted his mother to come back, but she never did. He was angry and he never forgot.

Barack listened to Sarah's stories about the family. Then, he went outside. Behind her house, under the ground, were his dead grandfather and father. Obama read his grandfather's name and dates. Next to this place was his father, but there was no name or dates. Did nobody love this man when he died? That was sad for Barack, and he cried. He understood more about his father's difficult life. His grandfather and father's life stories were now his story, too.

Years later, Auma told a London newspaper, "Barack has our father's hands. He moves them in the same way, and his handwriting is the same as our father's handwriting. He sits and talks in the same way, too."

In Kenya, Barack saw very, very poor people. He also saw beautiful hotels and expensive restaurants in Nairobi for the white visitors from rich countries. He saw wonderful wild animals away from the cities. His visit gave him a family, and it opened his eyes to a very different world.

In spring 1992, before Barack married Michelle Robinson in October, he took her to Kenya. She met his family and she, too, saw Africa for the first time. She wanted to see Nairobi's poorest people, so Auma and Barack took her to Kibera. Almost 1,000,000 very poor people live in two-and-a-half square kilometers. When Michelle saw the poor children, she cried. Before they left, they invited all of Obama's Kenyan family to Chicago for their important day in October.

When Barack and Michelle married, Roy, in his African clothes, stood next to his American brother. Roy was a Muslim at this time and he used his African name, Abongo. Barack's sister, brothers, aunts, and uncles from Kenya were there, too. Sadly, Michelle's father, Barack's grandfather, Stanley, and his mother's second husband, Lolo Soetoro, died before Barack and Michelle married. But Barack's mother flew to Chicago from Indonesia and Ann's mother, his grandmother, arrived from Hawaii. Obama's sister, Maya, was there, too.

Obama went to Africa again in August 2006, when he was a senator. He visited South Africa, and, at Robben Island, he stood inside the four walls of Nelson Mandela's small room. The South African government hated Mandela's political ideas. They did not want black people to live freely with white people. The government only freed Mandela in 1990, after twenty-seven years, and he won the presidential elections in 1994.

Obama then went to Kenya for six days and visited his family again. But by this time, Obama was famous in his father's country, so there were a lot of TV cameras and newspaper writers there. He met the president of Kenya and other important people in the government. He wanted the United States to do more for Africa.

Obama thinks about Mandela's years at Robben Island.

Chapter 5   Husband, Father, and Illinois Senator

When Obama finished Harvard Law School in 1991, law offices across the country wanted him to work for them. But Obama wanted to go back to Chicago and organize a voter campaign for the Democrats. They wanted to win the votes of more black voters for the 1992 elections. Obama organized a very large number of people, and he worked for no money. At the end of six months, there were more than 150,000 more black Democrat voters in the state of Illinois. Illinois voters elected the first black woman to the United States Senate, and in November, the Democrat Bill Clinton won the presidential election.

In 1992, Obama got a good job with some top lawyers in Chicago but the job did not pay as much as a lawyer's job with a very big company. So he started teaching at the Chicago Law School at the same time. Michelle, too, had a good job. Life was good for them. But they were not rich because they had to pay back the banks for their very expensive education at Harvard Law School.

Then, Obama began working on *Dreams from My Father*. He could get a lot of money from the book, he hoped. He wrote the story of his life—the life of a young black man in a white person's world. It is a story about race, and about a son's visit to his father's country. He wrote at night and slept only four hours.

Ann got sick in Indonesia, so she went back to Hawaii. Barack and Michelle visited her in the hospital. Ann's hair began to fall out. "But she will get better," Barack thought. She talked to her son about his book, and she helped him with some of it. Ann also talked to Barack about her money problems. Hospitals are expensive in the United States and this was a very difficult problem for many Americans. Obama talked about his mother when he campaigned for president. "When she was sick, she had to think about money. This is wrong," he told voters. He wanted to change the laws. He wanted the American government to help poorer sick people.

Barack and Michelle took some time away from their jobs. They went to Bali for some months and Barack finished his book. Then in 1995, a short time after it started selling in the bookstores, his mother died at the age of fifty-two. Barack often says, "The best things in me come from my mother."

At that time, Obama really wanted to be a politician. In 1996, he campaigned for the Illinois Senate and won. From 1997 to 2004, he worked hard for the people of Illinois but, at that time, the Republicans had more power. Obama worked with Democrats and Republicans. "Democrats and Republicans listened to his ideas carefully," Republican Senator Kirk Dillard said later.

Obama tried to help women, children, poor people, and old people. He wanted to change the laws on guns, too, because too many Americans had dangerous guns. He wanted to help young black men because white policemen stopped more black drivers than white drivers on the roads. In 2004, the Democrats had more power, with more Democrats than Republicans in the Senate, so change was possible.

Barack and Michelle had a daughter, Malia, in 1999 and a second daughter, Natasha in 2001. Michelle wanted her husband to help her with the children. But in 2000, Obama campaigned for another political job. Michelle was not happy because the campaign cost them a lot of money. "Everything went wrong in that campaign," Obama later wrote in his second book, *The Audacity of Hope*. After Obama lost, Michelle was sick of politics.

In October 2002, Obama spoke to 2,000 people in Chicago about President George W. Bush's plan for a war in Iraq. Obama wanted politicians to discuss other possible plans. He wanted Bush to wait, and he wanted the United States to work with other countries, not only Britain. Obama said, "Americans will have to stay in Iraq for years and it will cost a lot of money. The people in the Middle East will be angry at the United States, and some people there will want to kill more Americans." He did not vote with other senators for a war in Iraq.

Two years later, after Obama spoke to the Democrats in Boston, he was famous, not only in the United States but across the world. On that day, he spoke about hope: "Our fathers and grandfathers, mothers and grandmothers built this country with their hopes for their children's future. We can do the right thing and work for our children's future, too." In November 2004, voters in Illinois elected Obama to the United States Senate, so he went from the state senate to the country's senate.

Senator Obama moved to a small apartment in Washington, D.C., but his wife stayed in Chicago with their daughters. He was unhappy without his wife and daughters, so he went home for weekends. It was not an easy time for the Obama family.

In 2006, a lot of Americans read Obama's second book, and they started talking about Obama for president. "I can't try

Obama speaks to Democrats in Boston in July 2004.

now. It's too early—maybe later, in 2012 or 2016," he thought. But politics can change suddenly. And it did. Obama was in Ukraine when very bad weather hit the city of New Orleans in Louisiana in August 2005. A lot of poor people died, and most of them were black. Many Americans were angry because Bush's government did not send help to these poor people quickly. On TV Americans saw pictures of dead people face-down in water in the streets. Other people had no food, clothes, houses, or money. Obama, the only African-American senator, wanted to speak for the poor people there. In Washington, he spoke to all of the senators about the poor people in the United States. "They have guns but they do not have hope," he said. After that, many Americans wanted to hear more from Obama. They wanted him to be a presidential candidate.

Chapter 6 The Presidential Candidate

In Chicago in December 2006, Senator Obama discussed his future with political organizers David Axelrod, David Plouffe, and Steve Hildebrand. At that time, Obama liked his life and he did not have money problems. He and Michelle were in a bigger house in Chicago, and they loved time with their daughters. Axelrod asked Obama, "Can you walk away from that life and begin the very difficult life of a campaigner?" Obama had to ask his wife.

Michelle did not like politics. She lived her life for her family and community. But she did not say no. Michelle asked Axelrod and Plouffe a lot of questions. "Will I see him on the weekends?" she asked. Plouffe answered, "No." Then Michelle asked, "Can he win?" Hildebrand said, "Now is the time for Obama. In 2012, maybe it will be too late." Michelle told Barack, "We'll be fine. We're strong."

They went to Hawaii for Christmas, and Obama thought about

his future. When he went back to Washington, D.C., in January, he met with his political organizers. "You can plan the campaign," he said. "You don't *have to* do it," Axelrod told him. "I'll think about it for three or four more days," Obama answered. One week later, Obama told them, "You can start giving jobs to people."

On February 10, 2007, Obama told 15,000 people at the Illinois State House, "I am a Democratic candidate for the presidency." Suddenly, the presidential campaign was very exciting.

The number of Democratic candidates went down to only two—Hillary Clinton and Barack Obama. The others could not win and so they stopped campaigning. Three months before Election Day on November 4, 2007, one of them had to win more votes from Democrats in some important states. Iowa was one of them. There, Obama told people, "I want to win, but I don't only want to win. I want to change this country." In his Senate office he had pictures of Abraham Lincoln, Martin Luther King, and Mahatma Gandhi on the wall. Every day Obama looked at them and he saw hope for change. But Clinton, the first woman presidential candidate, wanted to change her country, too, and she fought a very strong campaign.

Obama and his people were younger than Clinton and her people. Young people and college students across the country made telephone calls to voters. Sometimes they made 25,000 calls in one day. They worked for no money. Obama's campaign was not very different from community organizing. People went from door to door and from church to church. The Clintons could sit and wait for their money; Obama had to work every day for his. Their votes in the Senate on the war in Iraq made Obama different from Clinton, too. She voted yes.

Obama's campaign was also different because he did not say bad things about Clinton or the Republicans. Politicians often play a game of dirty politics, so a lot of people liked Obama's way of campaigning. Also, Obama never got angry. Michelle says, "People

have to understand Hawaii. Then, they can understand Barack."
His early life in beautiful Hawaii with his young, intelligent mother
taught him important lessons about a quiet, disciplined life. Win
or lose, Obama does not get wild, angry, or very excited.

But Michelle is different. The Robinson family played games
at home when Michelle was a child. "Michelle really hates to
lose," Craig says about his sister. Michelle wanted her husband
to win in the important states, so she gave a lot of her time
to the campaign. When Obama lost the early vote in Texas,
she was angry. She told Plouffe and her husband, "Get some
new plans!" Back in Chicago, Obama told his workers, "I'm
not angry at you and I'm not shouting. But Texas cost us a lot of
money, and we have to do better next time."

Some people asked, "Is Obama really black? He went to white
schools and had a white family. And he's rich. What does he know
about the life of poor black people?" That made Michelle angry
because Barack understood the black community in Chicago. He
understood her family. "My parents, my brother, and I lived in
a one bedroom apartment in South Chicago. My mother stayed
home and my father worked for the city. They disciplined their
children and gave us a good education. But it was not easy,"
she said. Michelle spoke at colleges for black students and told
them about her husband. "My husband wants to help African-
Americans," she said. But Barack had a problem with some black
voters. When he spoke to large numbers of black workers, his wife
heard an educated law teacher, not a man of the people. He had to
use different words because these people were not law students.
Michelle helped him, and he started speaking differently.

Obama won in the state of Iowa, but Clinton won in New
Hampshire. But, in the end, Clinton lost. On August 27, the
Democrats had their first African-American presidential candidate.

So the fight between the Republican John McCain and
Obama began. On TV they discussed many important things,

and the economy was one of them. But one day is a long time in politics. Suddenly, on September 14, the Lehman Brothers Bank lost everything. Then, more American banks had problems. Suddenly, the economy was the most important problem in the country. A lot of Americans lost their jobs, their houses, and their money. The next president had to find ways out of this and many other problems. Which man could do it? McCain? He stopped campaigning and went back to Washington. He wanted to help the government, he said. But people asked, "Why did he suddenly leave the campaign? Was he afraid?" After that, Obama's campaign got stronger and stronger.

McCain tried to make voters afraid of Obama's ideas. "His economic ideas are not good for our country," McCain said. People smiled at Obama's answer. "McCain calls me names. What will he do next? Maybe he will call me a Communist because I gave some of my sandwich to other children in school."

On Election Night, November 4, 2008, on the thirty-sixth floor of a hotel in Chicago, the Obama family and some friends watched TV. David Mendell, a newspaperman from Chicago, was there, too. He later wrote about that night in his book about Obama. It was very exciting. Obama won in almost all of the most important states. Axelrod and Plouffe arrived. Plouffe took Obama in his arms, and Axelrod put out his hand to the next president. Michelle and her mother smiled.

Malia said to her dad, "You're the next president. What are you going to do first?"

"Buy a dog," Obama answered.

"No, the first political thing," his daughter asked, not happy with his answer.

There was no time for an answer because they had to go to Chicago's Grant Park. There, more than 200,000 people and a lot of TV cameramen waited for their next president. The Obama family walked out hand-in-hand in front of them.

23

Michelle and their daughters sat down. After Obama spoke, the family left for a big party.

Before Axelrod left, he saw some African-American children with wet eyes. He started crying, too, because he remembered Obama's words to Michelle about black people two years before. At that time, Obama told his wife, "When I am president, the world will look at us differently. *That* is something."

The Obama family at Grant Park on November 4, 2008.

ACTIVITIES

Chapters 1–2

Before you read

1 What do you know about African-Americans? What do you know about Barack Obama?

2 Look at the twenty words in the Word List at the back of the book.
   a Which are words for people?
   b Change these words into words for people. What do those people do?
   vote   campaign   organize   law   politics   senate

3 Read the Introduction. Answer these questions.
   a What were Obama's jobs before he was president?
   b What more do you know about Obama now?
   c Why did Obama's mother teach him about Martin Luther King, Nelson Mandela, and Mahatma Gandhi, do you think?

While you read

4 Write the dates.
   a Obama started the first four years of his
     presidency.   ....
   b President Abraham Lincoln started his
     presidency.   ....
   c The American North fought the South
     in a great war.   ....
   d Martin Luther King spoke to more than 250,000. ....

5 Which of these did Obama talk about on January 20, 2009? Check (✓) the right answers.
   a the American dream   ......
   b the economy   ......
   c the wars in Iraq and Afghanistan   .....
   d sick people without money for hospitals   ......
   e bad schools for children in poor families   ......

6 Where did these happen? Write the names of the places.
   a Barack Obama, Sr. worked on his father's farm ....
   b Obama Sr. and his wife, Ann, had a son.   ....
   c Obama Sr. studied at Harvard.   ....

d Ann and Barry lived with her new husband,
Lolo. ....

e Barry went to a very good American school. ....

After you read

7 Discuss Obama's early education from his mother, his schools,
and his life at home. Did this help him later in life, do you think?
Or did his early education make his life more difficult?

Chapters 3–4

Before you read

8 Look at the names of Chapters 3 and 4 and the photos in those
chapters. What did Obama do next, do you think?

9 Did Obama meet his father again, do you think? Did Obama
want to learn about his Kenyan family? Why (not)?

While you read

10 Here are some people in Obama's life. Match the words
below with the right people.

a Jerry Kellman ......

b Auma Obama ......

c Barack Obama, Sr. ......

d Craig Robinson ......

   1) learned about Obama from a basketball game

   2) died in a car accident

   3) gave Obama a community organizer's job in Chicago

   4) visited Obama in Chicago and told him about his father

11 Write the right name or names from Barack Obama, Sr.'s
family.

a She is Obama Sr.'s first wife. ....

b They are Auma's three brothers. ....

....

c He is the son of Obama Sr. and his
third wife, Ruth. ....

d He was Obama Sr.'s son but he
died in a car accident in 1983. ....

e He is Obama Sr.'s youngest son. ....

f He was Obama Sr.'s father. ....

After you read

12 Discuss these questions.

    a In what ways was Onyango's life the same as Barack Obama, Sr.'s life?

    b In what ways was Barack Obama, Sr.'s life the same as his son's life? In what ways is President Obama the same as his father?

13 Why were these important in Obama's life?

    a South Chicago   b Harvard Law School   c Kogelo

14 In Kenya, and other countries, some men have more than one wife. Is this good for families, do you think? Why (not)?

Chapters 5–6

Before you read

15 Look at the names of Chapters 5–6. Discuss these questions.

    a How did Obama's life change after he finished at Harvard, do you think?

    b Did Michelle's life change very much, do you think? Why (not)?

While you read

16 What happened first? And then? Write the numbers 1–8.

    a Obama got a lawyer's job and started teaching at Chicago Law School. ......

    b Obama's book started selling and his mother died. ......

    c Obama was famous after he spoke to Democrats in Boston in 2004. ......

    d Obama's voter campaign ended with 150,000 more black voters in Illinois. ......

    e Obama began working on *Dreams from My Father.* ......

    f Obama and Michelle had two daughters. ......

    g Obama won the election for the Illinois Senate. ......

    h Ann got sick in Indonesia and went back to Hawaii. ......

17 Did Obama win these? Write *won* or *lost*.

    a the 1996 election for Illinois state senator ....

    b the 2000 campaign for a political job ....

    c the 2004 election for United States senator ....

    d the vote in Texas for the Democratic candidate ....

    e the 2008 campaign for the Democratic candidate ....

After you read

18 Who said this? What did they mean?
- **a** "You can start giving jobs to people."
- **b** "People have to understand Hawaii. Then, they can understand Barack."
- **c** "When I am president, the world will look at us differently. *That* is something."

Writing

19 On January 20, 2009, Obama said, "A country cannot be rich when the government helps only rich people." Was he right? What do you think? Write your ideas about this for a newspaper in your country.

20 Obama used the words "Hope," "Change," and "Yes we can" in his presidential campaign. Write a letter from presidential candidate Barack Obama to a Washington newspaper. Why are you using these words in your campaign? Why do people want to hear them?

21 Write a letter to a friend about the life of Onyango, Obama's grandfather. Was it an interesting life, do you think?

22 Write a letter to President Obama. Ask him questions about his first visit to Kenya. Ask him about his family there.

23 Write a conversation between Barack and Michelle after he starts working with her. He wants to take her to a movie or a restaurant but she does not want to go out with him.

24 You want to make a movie about Obama's life—the good times and the bad times. What is the name of the movie? Who will play Barack and Michelle Obama in the movie? Put your ideas and some pictures or photos on paper.

Answers for the activities in the book are available from the Penguin Readers website. A free Activity Worksheet is also available from the website. Activity Worksheets are part of the Penguin Teacher Support Programme, which also includes Progress Tests and Graded Reader Guidelines. For more information, please visit:
www.penguinreaders.com.